SEEN

Embracing the Girl God Sees

A Guided Devotional for Youg women and teen girls

Written by Shabriya Hill O

OnaHillPublishing.com

To every girl who wonders if she matters — you do.

Dear Beautiful Girl,

Life as a teen can be a whirlwind of emotions, questions, and discoveries. Amidst the noise of the world, it's easy to forget who you truly are and the incredible purpose you hold.
This 30-day devotional is crafted just for you—to remind you daily of your worth, guide you through your emotions, strengthen your faith, and help you uncover your God-given purpose.

Each day offers a Scripture to anchor your heart, a reflection to ponder, a question to challenge you, and a prayer to draw you closer to God. You are not alone on this journey. Let's walk together, day by day, discovering the depth of God's love for you.

With love and prayers,

Shabriya Hill O

How to Use This Devotional

This devotional is your personal space to grow in faith, hear from God, and be reminded daily that you are loved. Here's how to make the most of these next 30 days.

1. Set Aside Daily Time

Choose a quiet time that works best for you—whether it's in the morning before school, at lunch, or before bed. Even 10–15 minutes a day with God can change everything.

2. Open Your Bible

Each day includes a Bible verse. While it's written on the page, looking it up in your own Bible helps you learn where things are and lets you see the full context. Don't be afraid to underline or highlight what stands out!

3. Read the Devotion Thoughtfully

Start with the Scripture. Then read the short devotional. Imagine God speaking right to your heart through those words—because He is.

4. Reflect and Journal

At the end of each devotional, you'll find a reflection question. Take time to think about it. Write your thoughts in a notebook or journal. This helps you see what God is teaching you.

5. Talk to God in Prayer

Each day includes a prayer you can say out loud or in your heart. Then feel free to add your own words. God loves hearing from you—especially when you're honest and real.

6. Revisit or Reread

Some days may speak more strongly than others. That's okay! Go back to your favorite days anytime. You might find new meaning the second or third time around.

7. Share with a Friend

You don't have to walk this journey alone. Invite a friend to do the devotional with you. Talk about what God is teaching you both and encourage one another.

Remember:

This devotional isn't about being perfect. It's about being real and making space for God in your everyday life. He's already waiting to meet with you—just show up.

WEEK 1

IDENTITY

"See what great love the Father has lavished on us, that we should be called children of God! And that is what we are!"

— 1 John 3:1 (NIV)

Day 1 – You Are Seen

Key Verse

"You are the God who sees me." – Genesis 16:13 (NIV)

Devotional Thought

Have you ever walked into a room and felt completely invisible? Like no one notices you, no one's looking for you, and no one really cares if you're there or not? That's how Hagar felt in the Bible. She was mistreated, alone, and running away. But then God showed up. Not only did He speak to her, He gave her a promise—and in that moment, she realized something powerful: God saw her.

You might not be running away in the desert like Hagar, but maybe you've been hiding how you really feel. Maybe you're overwhelmed by expectations, friendships that hurt, or just feeling like you'll never be "enough." The truth is, even when no one else sees what you're going through—God does.

He doesn't overlook your pain, your tears, or your silent prayers at night. He sees it all. And not in a "watching-from-far-away" kind of way, but in a "close, caring, involved" kind of way.

So, next time you feel invisible, remember Genesis 16:13. Say it out loud: "God sees me." Because He truly does.

Reflect

- When was a time you felt unseen or overlooked?
- How does it change things to know that God sees you—even the parts you hide from others?

Prayer Moment

God, thank You for seeing me. Even when I feel invisible, You know my heart. Help me believe that I matter to You every single day. Amen.

My Notes & Prayers

_____

_____

_____

_____

_____

_____

_____

_____

_____

_____

_____

_____

_____

_____

Day 2 – You Are Not Alone

Key Verse

"Never will I leave you; never will I forsake you." –
Hebrews 13:5b (NIV)

Devotional Thought

It's weird how you can be in a crowded school hallway, surrounded by people, and still feel completely alone. Like no one really gets you. Maybe your best friend has drifted away, or maybe you've been smiling on the outside while crying on the inside.

God knows that loneliness. Jesus experienced it too—He was betrayed, abandoned, and even misunderstood by people close to Him. So when He promises that He'll never leave you, He means it. He's not going anywhere.

Even in your most silent or darkest moments, God is present. You don't have to say the right words or pretend to be okay. Just be real with Him. He can handle your sadness, confusion, and questions.

The world may feel loud and disconnected, but God's voice is steady, gentle, and near. He says, "I'm here. I haven't left. I never will."

Reflect

- When have you felt the most alone?
- What does it mean to you that God will never leave?

Prayer Moment

Jesus, sometimes I feel like I'm the only one going through this. Help me remember that You are always with me—even when I feel alone. Amen.

My Notes & Prayers

_____

_____

_____

_____

_____

_____

_____

_____

_____

_____

_____

_____

_____

_____

Day 3 – You Are Enough

Key Verse
"I praise you because I am fearfully and wonderfully made; your works are wonderful, I know that full well." – Psalm 139:14 (NIV)

Devotional Thought
There's a lie that's really easy to believe: "I'm not enough."
Not pretty enough. Not smart enough. Not spiritual enough.

Social media, comparison, and even comments from people you love can make it feel like you're constantly falling short.

But here's the truth: God made you on purpose, with purpose. You are not a mistake. You don't have to "fix" yourself to earn His love. You're already enough in His eyes because He created you with intention, beauty, and strength.

Psalm 139 reminds you that you're fearfully and wonderfully made. That means you were crafted with care and awe by the Creator of the universe.

He looks at you and sees value—not because of your looks, grades, or achievements—but because you are His daughter. You might not feel "enough" today, but feelings aren't facts.

God's Word is the truth, and it says you are wonderfully made.

Reflect

- What areas of your life make you feel "not enough"?
- How can you start replacing those lies with God's truth?

Prayer Moment

Father, help me believe what You say about me. Remind me that I am wonderfully made, loved, and enough—just as I am. Amen.

My Notes & Prayers

_____

_____

_____

_____

_____

_____

_____

_____

_____

_____

_____

_____

_____

_____

Day 4: You Are Chosen

Key Verse
"But you are a chosen people, a royal priesthood, a holy nation, God's special possession, that you may declare the praises of him who called you out of darkness into his wonderful light."
– 1 Peter 2:9 (NIV)

Devotional Thought
There's something powerful about being chosen. Whether it's being picked for a team, invited to a party, or asked to lead something important, it feels good to be selected. It reminds you that you matter.

But what happens when you're not picked? When you feel invisible, overlooked, or forgotten? It can make you question your value.

Here's the truth you can hold onto today: God chose you—on purpose, with purpose, and for a purpose. Long before you were born, He saw you. He knew your name, your personality, your struggles, and your story. And still, He said, "She's mine."

You weren't chosen because you're perfect or because you've got it all figured out. You were chosen because God's love for you is that deep, that real, and that personal.

He doesn't make random choices. You are part of His royal family, set apart to shine His light in a world that desperately needs it.

When you feel left out, remind yourself: You are not overlooked by God. When insecurity whispers that you don't belong, remember: You were chosen by the One who made the universe.

You don't have to chase approval when you're already chosen.
You don't have to pretend to be someone else when God already picked you.

So, walk confidently. You are His.

Reflect
- What areas of your life make you feel left out, unwanted or less than?
- How does knowing you are chosen by God shift your confidence and identity?

Prayer Moment
Father, thank You for never forgetting me. Help me to trust that You are always near, even when I feel alone. Amen.

My Notes & Prayers

_____

_____

_____

_____

_____

_____

_____

_____

_____

_____

_____

_____

_____

_____

Day 5: You Are Not Forgotten

Key Verse
"See, I have engraved you on the palms of my hands; your walls are ever before me." – Isaiah 49:16 (NIV)

Devotional Thought
Have you ever felt invisible? Like if you disappeared for a day, no one would even notice?

Maybe your texts go unanswered, your posts get ignored, or you walk into a room and feel like no one sees you. It's easy to feel forgotten in a world full of noise, comparison, and filters.

But God sees you.

Not just when you're on your best behavior or when you're being strong. He sees you when you're curled up in bed crying, when you feel overwhelmed at school, and when you're silently wondering if you even matter.

God says, "I have engraved you on the palms of My hands." That means He's got a permanent reminder of you. You're not written in pencil that can be erased.

You're engraved—etched into His love, never forgotten, never ignored, and never overlooked.

This verse was originally written to God's people when they were feeling abandoned. They thought God had left them. But He responded with love, reminding them—and you—that He never stops thinking about you. You are always on His mind.

Even when you don't feel it, God is working behind the scenes for your good. He sees the pain you haven't told anyone about. He understands the loneliness. He's holding you close—even if it feels quiet.

You are remembered.
You are treasured.
You are never, ever forgotten.

Reflect

- Have you recently felt unseen or left out?
- How does knowing God has "engraved" you on His hands give you comfort today?

Prayer Moment

God, sometimes I feel so small and forgotten. Thank You for reminding me that You see me and that I'm always on Your heart. Help me to remember Your love when I feel alone. Let me rest in the truth that I matter to You—deeply and personally.   Amen.

My Notes & Prayers

_____

_____

_____

_____

_____

_____

_____

_____

_____

_____

_____

_____

_____

_____

Day 6: You Are a Daughter of the King

Key Verse

"The Spirit you received does not make you slaves, so that you live in fear again; rather, the Spirit you received brought about your adoption to sonship. And by him we cry, 'Abba, Father.' The Spirit himself testifies with our spirit that we are God's children. Now if we are children, then we are heirs—heirs of God and co-heirs with Christ..." —Romans 8:15–17a (NIV)

Devotional Thought

When you think of royalty, what comes to mind? Fancy dresses, sparkling crowns, grand palaces, and red carpets?

Now pause. What if I told you that you're royalty too?

You might not live in a palace or wear a crown, but the Bible says you are a daughter of the King—God, the Creator of the universe. That makes you more than just someone trying to survive high school or figure out your future. It makes you royalty with a purpose.

When God adopted you into His family through Jesus, He didn't do it reluctantly or by accident. He wanted you. He chose you. And now, you don't live as a slave to fear, insecurity, or shame—you live as His child. His daughter.

That means you have access to His love, His strength, and His promises. You have a spiritual inheritance. You are protected, guided, and deeply loved—not because of anything you've earned, but because of who your Father is.

And here's the amazing part: as His daughter, you can call Him "Abba"—a close, intimate word that means "Daddy." The King of heaven wants that kind of closeness with you.

You don't have to prove your worth. You already have it. You don't have to fight for a place at the table. You already have a seat.
You don't have to wonder if you belong. You already do.

So lift your head high, daughter. Not in pride, but in holy confidence. Because your identity isn't in what others say—it's in who your Father is.

Reflect
- What would change if you truly believed you are royalty in God's eyes?
- Are there lies you've believed about your identity that God wants to replace with truth?

Prayer Moment

Father God, thank You for adopting me into Your family. Help me live like the daughter of a King—not with fear or shame, but with confidence in who You say I am. Let me walk in Your truth and represent You with love, grace, and courage.

Amen.

My Notes & Prayers

_____

_____

_____

_____

_____

_____

_____

_____

_____

_____

_____

_____

_____

DAY 7: You Are Valuable

Key Verse

"So don't be afraid; you are worth more than many sparrows." — Matthew 10:31 (NIV)

Devotional Thought

Sometimes it's easy to feel overlooked, underestimated, or not enough. In a world that often measures value by popularity, appearance, or achievements, you might wonder: Do I really matter?

But Jesus answers that question with a beautiful, powerful yes.

In Matthew 10:31, Jesus tells His followers not to be afraid. Why? Because they are deeply known and treasured by God. He even says that God knows every hair on your head! That means your value isn't based on what others think—your value comes from the One who created you.

God made you on purpose, for a purpose. He designed your smile, your heart, your personality. You are not a mistake. You are not too much or not enough. You are God's masterpiece.

And just like sparrows—small, ordinary birds—are cared for by God, how much more will He care for you, His beloved daughter?

Let this truth sink deep into your heart: You are valuable. Not because of what you do or how you feel, but because of who you belong to.

Reflect

- What voices in your life have made you question your worth, and how does God's Word speak a different truth?
- What would change about your day if you fully believed, deep down, that you are precious to God?

Prayer Moment

God, sometimes I forget how much I matter to You. Thank You for creating me with love and calling me valuable. Help me to see myself through Your eyes and to walk in confidence, knowing I am chosen, cherished, and deeply loved. Amen.

Bonus Journaling Prompt

God says I am valuable. Today, I will believe it by...

My Notes & Prayers

_____

_____

_____

_____

_____

_____

_____

_____

_____

_____

_____

_____

_____

_____

_____ / _____ / _____

Weekly Check-in

How I felt this week,

_____

_____

_____

_____

_____

_____

_____

_____

_____

_____

_____

_____

_____

Identity Activity: "Who God Says I Am" Mirror Craft

Purpose:

To help teen girls see themselves the way God sees them—loved, chosen, valuable, and purposeful.

Supplies Needed:

- Small handheld mirrors (or cardstock cutouts shaped like mirrors)
- Markers, pens, or colored pencils
- Decorative items: stickers, washi tape, rhinestones, lace, glitter, etc.
- Printed Bible verses about identity (optional)
- Glue, scissors

Instructions:

1. Decorate the Mirror Frame:
2. Use a mirror or a cardstock cutout. Have them decorate it with their favorite colors, patterns, or embellishments. Encourage creativity—it should reflect them.
3. Write Truths Around the Frame:
4. Around the mirror, write identity truths like:
    - "I am loved."
    - "I am chosen."
    - "I am enough."
    - "I am a daughter of the King."
    - "I am forgiven."
    - "I am strong."
    - "I am created for a purpose."
5. (Add a list of verses like Ephesians 2:10, 1 Peter 2:9, Romans 8:38–39, Psalm 139:14.)
6. Reflection Moment:
7. Look into your mirror and say one truth out loud, like:
8. "God, thank You for making me wonderfully. I am Yours."
9. You can also play soft worship music and reflect or pray quietly.

WEEK 2:

EMOTIONS

"Why, my soul, are you downcast? Why so disturbed within me? Put your hope in God, for I will yet praise him, my Savior and my God."

— Psalm 42:11 (NIV)

DAY 8: When You Feel Anxious

Key Verse
"Do not be anxious about anything, but in every situation, by prayer and petition, with thanksgiving, present your requests to God. And the peace of God, which transcends all understanding, will guard your hearts and your minds in Christ Jesus." — Philippians 4:6–7 (NIV)

Devotional Thought
Anxiety can sneak in like a storm—racing thoughts, tight chest, and a heart that won't slow down. Whether it's a big test, a friend issue, or the unknown future, feeling anxious is something every girl faces. But you don't have to face it alone.

Philippians 4 reminds you that you can bring everything —yes, everything—to God. He's not too busy or bothered by your worries. In fact, He wants you to tell Him about them. When you talk to Him in prayer and thank Him for what He's already done, something amazing happens: peace.

Not just any peace, but God's peace. A peace that doesn't always make sense, but calms you anyway. It's like a blanket that wraps around your heart and mind, guarding you from the lies that try to take over.

You don't have to pretend everything's okay. Just be honest with God, and let Him trade your anxiety for His peace.

Reflect
- What's been making you anxious lately?
- Take a moment to tell God about it, and ask Him to fill you with His peace.

Prayer Moment
God, You already know what's making me anxious. Help me to trust You with the things I can't control. Thank You for always listening. Fill my heart with Your peace today and remind me that I'm never alone. Amen

My Notes & Prayers

_____

_____

_____

_____

_____

_____

_____

_____

_____

_____

_____

_____

_____

DAY 9: When You Feel Angry

Key Verse

"My dear brothers and sisters, take note of this: Everyone should be quick to listen, slow to speak and slow to become angry, because human anger does not produce the righteousness that God desires."
— James 1:19–20 (NIV)

Devotional Thought

Anger isn't a sin. Anger is a powerful emotion. It can flare up when someone hurts you, when things feel unfair, or when no one seems to understand. And while feeling angry isn't wrong—God gave us emotions—how we respond to anger matters.

James tells us to be quick to listen, slow to speak, and slow to become angry. Why? Because when we act out of anger, we usually make things worse, not better. Yelling, snapping, or holding a grudge won't bring peace—it pulls us further away from the kind of person God wants us to be.

So, what can you do when you feel angry?

Stop and breathe. Talk to God about it.
Ask Him to help you listen, speak with kindness, and respond with love—even when it's hard.
God understands your anger, and He wants to help you through it—not shame you for it.

Reflect

What situations or people tend to make you angry? Think of a time you got angry and reacted in a way you regretted. What could you do differently next time with God's help?

Prayer Moment

God, You know when my heart feels overwhelmed with anger. Help me to pause, listen, and respond with grace. Teach me to handle my emotions in a way that honors You. I want to be more like You, even when it's hard.
   Amen.

My Notes & Prayers

_____

_____

_____

_____

_____

_____

_____

_____

_____

_____

_____

_____

_____

_____

DAY 10: When You Feel Sad

Key Verse

"The Lord is close to the brokenhearted and saves those who are crushed in spirit." — Psalm 34:18 (NIV)

Devotional Thought

Sadness can feel heavy. Sometimes it's caused by something obvious—like losing a friend, being hurt, or feeling left out. Other times, you're just sad and you don't even know why. No matter the reason, God cares deeply about your broken heart.

Psalm 34:18 reminds you that God is close when you're hurting. He doesn't back away from your tears—He draws near. Even when it feels like no one understands or no one sees what you're going through, God does. He sees every tear, every silent cry, every ache in your heart.

Jesus Himself knew what it felt like to be sad. So you never have to hide your emotions from Him. You can cry, be honest, and let Him comfort you. His love is strong enough to carry your pain, and gentle enough to heal your heart. He's not afraid of your feelings—He's with you through them all.

Reflect

- What is one small step you can take today to let God's comfort into your heart?
- How might your sadness become part of a beautiful story He's writing in your life?

Prayer Moment

Lord, thank You for being close to me when I'm hurting. Sometimes my sadness feels too big to handle, but You promise to stay near. Please comfort my heart and help me feel Your presence. I trust You with my emotions. Amen.

My Notes & Prayers

_____

_____

_____

_____

_____

_____

_____

_____

_____

_____

_____

_____

_____

DAY 11: When You Feel Left Out

Key Verse

"Though my father and mother forsake me, the Lord will receive me." — Psalm 27:10 (NIV)

Devotional Thought

Being left out hurts. Whether it's not getting invited, being ignored in a group chat, or watching friends make plans without you—it can make you feel invisible, unwanted, and rejected. But God wants you to know something powerful: you are never left out with Him.

Psalm 27:10 reminds us that even if the people closest to us walk away, God never will. He's not just with you— He welcomes you. He receives you with open arms, every time.

Your value isn't defined by who includes you in their group—it's defined by the One who chose you before the world began.

You belong to Him. You are seen, known, and loved—no matter what anyone else says or does.
He always includes you. Even when others forget you, He never does. You belong to Him. And in His family, you always have a place.

Reflect
- Have you ever felt forgotten or excluded?
- When others leave you out, how can you lean into the truth that God always includes you?
- What does it mean to you that God will never leave you?
- What might God be inviting you to do with the love and confidence He gives you?

Prayer Moment

God, sometimes it really hurts to feel left out. But thank You for always including me and reminding me that I always belong with You. Help me to remember that I'm never alone because I belong to You and to find my worth in You, not in others' opinions. Use this moment to draw me closer to You and show me who I really am—chosen and loved.

   Amen.

My Notes & Prayers

_____

_____

_____

_____

_____

_____

_____

_____

_____

_____

_____

_____

_____

_____

DAY 12: When You Feel Insecure

Key Verse

"But he said to me, 'My grace is sufficient for you, for my power is made perfect in weakness.'
Therefore I will boast all the more gladly about my weaknesses, so that Christ's power may rest on me."
— 2 Corinthians 12:9–10 (NIV)

Devotional Thought

Insecurity can show up in quiet whispers—"You're not pretty enough." "You're not good enough." "You'll never measure up." It makes you compare, question, and shrink back. But those voices aren't from God.

God doesn't ask you to be perfect. He invites you to bring your weakness to Him—and promises that His power shows up best there. The very things you think make you "not enough" are the exact places where God's grace can shine the brightest. God's strength shines through our weaknesses. You don't have to have it all together. You don't need to look like her, talk like her, or be like anyone else. You are His. masterpiece, and when you feel insecure, that's your moment to lean into His strength.
You don't have to be perfect—God's power works best in your imperfection. That means even your flaws can show His goodness.

Reflect
- What's one insecurity you've been holding onto?
- How can you give it to God today?
- What if your weakness is the exact place where God wants to show His strength?
- How can you start seeing yourself through His eyes today?

Prayer Moment
Lord, sometimes I feel like I'm not enough. But You say Your grace is all I need. Help me to stop comparing and start trusting that You created me on purpose. Let Your strength shine through every place I feel weak.
Amen.

My Notes & Prayers

_____

_____

_____

_____

_____

_____

_____

_____

_____

_____

_____

_____

_____

_____

DAY 13: When You're Overwhelmed

Key Verse
"When you pass through the waters, I will be with you; and when you pass through the rivers, they will not sweep over you. When you walk through the fire, you will not be burned; the flames will not set you ablaze." — Isaiah 43:2 (NIV)

Devotional Thought
Life can get overwhelming—fast. Between school, friendships, family pressure, your future, and trying to be everything to everyone, it can feel like you're drowning. But here's the hope: God never promised we wouldn't face hard things—but He did promise we'd never face them alone.

Isaiah 43:2 doesn't say if you go through deep waters or fire—it says when. Life will have those moments. But God promises that even in the middle of the chaos, He will hold you steady. You will not be swept away. You will not be consumed.

When it feels like too much, remember: the One who created the universe walks with you. He's holding your hand through every wave and flame. Take a breath. You're not alone—and you're stronger than you think with Him by your side.

Reflect
What's overwhelming you right now? What would it look like to hand it over to God today and trust that He's walking through it with you? When has God brought you through something hard before? How can remembering that give you courage for what you're facing now?

Prayer Moment
God, sometimes everything feels like too much. I'm tired, stressed, and unsure what to do. Please help me breathe, trust, and remember that You are with me in every moment. Thank You for never letting me face the hard things alone. Amen.

My Notes & Prayers

_____

_____

_____

_____

_____

_____

_____

_____

_____

_____

_____

_____

_____

DAY 14: When You Need Peace

Key Verse

"Peace I leave with you; my peace I give you. I do not give to you as the world gives. Do not let your hearts be troubled and do not be afraid." — John 14:27 (NIV)

Devotional Thought

When your heart feels like it's racing, your thoughts won't stop spinning, or everything around you feels loud and unsettled—you need peace. But not the kind of peace the world offers through distractions or temporary fixes. You need the kind of peace that comes from Jesus.

In John 14:27, Jesus promises to leave His peace with you. This isn't a peace that depends on perfect circumstances. It's a deep, quiet confidence that you're loved, held, and safe—even in the middle of chaos.

Jesus knew His followers would face fear, anxiety, and confusion. That's why He gave them (and you) something better than just calm feelings—He gave His very own peace. It's steady. It's strong. And it never leaves you.

You don't have to wait for everything to be okay to feel okay. Peace is a gift—and today, you can choose to receive it.

Reflect

- What's been stealing your peace lately, and how can you invite Jesus into that space today?
- What would it look like to carry Jesus' peace with you—at school, at home, or even in your thoughts?

Prayer Moment

Jesus, thank You for offering me real peace—not the kind that disappears, but the kind that stays. Help me to trust that no matter what's going on around me, You are with me. Quiet my heart and fill me with Your perfect peace today.

Amen.

My Notes & Prayers

_____

_____

_____

_____

_____

_____

_____

_____

_____

_____

_____

_____

_____

_____

_____

Weekly Check-in

How I felt this week, _____

_____

_____

_____

_____

_____

_____

_____

_____

_____

_____

_____

_____

_____

Emotions Activity: "Heart Check with God"

Theme Verse:
"Cast all your anxiety on Him because He cares for you." —
1 Peter 5:7 (NIV)

Purpose:
To help girls name their emotions, understand they are not
alone in them, and learn to bring their feelings to God in
prayer.

Supplies Needed:
- Printable emotion cards or emojis (happy, sad, anxious,
  angry, joyful, confused, excited, etc.)
- Pen and paper or journal
- Colored pencils or markers
- Small envelopes or heart-shaped pockets (optional)

Instructions:
1. Pick a Feeling:
2. Choose a card or draw a face that represents how
   you're feeling today. Don't overthink it—just go with
   what's most true right now.
3. Ask Yourself:
   ○ Why do I feel this way?
   ○ What happened today or this week that brought up
     this feeling?
   ○ Have I talked to God about it?
4. Write It Out: In your journal or on a slip of paper, write:
   ○ "Today, I feel _____."
   ○ "God, this feeling is real. Please help me to
     _____."
   ○ Add a short prayer or a verse that comforts you.

- Tuck It in the Heart:
- Place your paper in the envelope or heart-shaped pocket labeled "Given to God." (Optional: Decorate your pocket with the verse 1 Peter 5:7.)
- Repeat Regularly:
- Make this a habit—whenever you feel overwhelmed, anxious, or excited, do a Heart Check with God. This will teach you to be honest with Him and let Him meet you in every emotion.

Bonus Reflection Prompt:
"How does it help to know that God cares about every feeling I have—even the ones I don't like?"

My Notes & Prayers

_____

_____

_____

_____

_____

_____

_____

_____

_____

_____

_____

_____

_____

_____

WEEK 3:

Faith

"'Have faith in God,' Jesus answered. 'Truly I tell you, if anyone says to this mountain, "Go, throw yourself into the sea," and does not doubt in their heart but believes that what they say will happen, it will be done for them. Therefore I tell you, whatever you ask for in prayer, believe that you have received it, and it will be yours.'" **Mark 11:22–24 (NIV)**

DAY 15: Trusting God's Plan

Key Verse

"Trust in the Lord with all your heart and lean not on your own understanding; in all your ways submit to him, and he will make your paths straight." — Proverbs 3:5–6 (NIV)

Devotional Thought

Sometimes life just doesn't make sense. Maybe your plans didn't work out, your prayers feel unanswered, or you're wondering what God is doing. It's hard to trust when the future feels blurry. But Proverbs 3:5–6 is a gentle reminder that you don't have to figure it all out.

God sees the full picture—even the parts you can't. He's not asking you to understand everything. He's asking you to trust Him with everything.

When you let go of control and give your plans to God, He promises to guide you. Not always in the way you expected, but always in the way that's best. Trust is choosing to believe that His way is higher, even when it's hard to see.

You don't have to have all the answers—you just need to hold the hand of the One who does.

Reflect

- What part of your life feels uncertain right now, and how can you choose to trust God with it today?
- How have you seen God work things out in the past—even when you didn't understand what He was doing at first?

Prayer Moment

God, I don't always understand what You're doing, but I want to trust You. Help me let go of the pressure to figure it all out. Show me how to lean on You with my whole heart. Guide me one step at a time, and help me follow wherever You lead. Amen.

My Notes & Prayers

_____

_____

_____

_____

_____

_____

_____

_____

_____

_____

_____

_____

_____

_____

DAY 16: Walking by Faith

Key Verse
"For we live by faith, not by sight." — 2 Corinthians 5:7 (NIV)

Devotional Thought
Walking by faith can feel scary. It means taking steps without knowing exactly where you're going or how things will turn out. It means choosing to trust God, even when you can't see the whole path.

But that's what faith is—believing that God is who He says He is, and that He'll do what He's promised, even when your feelings or circumstances say otherwise. Faith isn't about having all the answers—it's about trusting the One who does.

Think of it like walking in the dark while holding your Father's hand. You may not see what's ahead, but if you know who's leading you, you can keep walking.

Faith doesn't remove fear completely, but it gives you the courage to move forward anyway—step by step, with your heart fixed on Jesus.

Reflect
- What part of your life feels uncertain right now, and how can you choose to trust God with it today?
- How have you seen God work things out in the past—even when you didn't understand what He was doing at first?

Prayer Moment
God, I don't always understand what You're doing, but I want to trust You. Help me let go of the pressure to figure it all out. Show me how to lean on You with my whole heart. Guide me one step at a time, and help me follow wherever You lead.

Amen.

_____ / _____ / _____

My Notes & Prayers

_____

_____

_____

_____

_____

_____

_____

_____

_____

_____

_____

_____

_____

_____

_____

DAY 17: Hearing God's Voice

Key Verse
"My sheep listen to my voice; I know them, and they follow me." — John 10:27 (NIV)

Devotional Thought
In a world full of noise—social media, opinions, expectations—it can be hard to know which voice to follow. But Jesus says His sheep (that's you!) know His voice. That means you can hear Him.

God speaks in different ways—through His Word, through prayer, through a quiet nudge in your heart, or even through the words of someone else. But the more time you spend with Him, the easier it becomes to recognize His voice above all the rest.

Hearing God isn't about being perfect. It's about being close. Just like you learn the voice of a friend by spending time together, you learn God's voice by drawing near to Him. And the best part? He wants to speak to you.

So don't be discouraged if it takes time. Keep listening. Keep leaning in.

He knows you, He loves you, and He's always speaking.
He's not silent. He's speaking. Are you listening?

Reflect
- How can you create more quiet space in your day to hear God's voice clearly?
- What are some ways you've sensed God speaking to you in the past?

Prayer Moment
Jesus, sometimes it's hard to hear Your voice through all the noise in my life. Help me slow down, listen, and trust that You are speaking. Teach me to recognize Your voice and follow You with confidence.

Amen.

My Notes & Prayers

_____

_____

_____

_____

_____

_____

_____

_____

_____

_____

_____

_____

_____

_____

DAY 18: When God Feels Distant

Key Verse

"How long, Lord? Will you forget me forever? How long will you hide your face from me? How long must I wrestle with my thoughts and day after day have sorrow in my heart?" — Psalm 13:1–2 (NIV)

Devotional Thought

Have you ever prayed and felt like no one was listening? Or gone through something hard and wondered where God was? You're not alone. Even David—called a man after God's heart—felt like God was distant at times.

Psalm 13 is full of raw honesty. David asks hard questions, the kind you might feel too guilty to say out loud. But here's the amazing part: God included this in the Bible to remind you that it's okay to bring your confusion, pain, and questions to Him.

Faith doesn't mean you never feel distant from God. Faith means you keep talking to Him—even in the silence. And just because you feel far from God doesn't mean He's gone. He's still near, still working, still loving you—especially in the waiting.

You may not understand everything right now, but God sees your heart and holds every tear. He's not scared of your questions. He welcomes them—and He welcomes you.

Reflect

- When God feels far away, how can you remind yourself that He's still close and still cares?
- What do you do when God feels distant? How can you draw near to Him today?
- What would it look like to be honest with God about your feelings and trust Him with your doubts?

Prayer Moment

God, sometimes I feel like You're far away, and I don't understand why. But I choose to keep reaching for You. Help me trust that You are still with me, even when I can't feel You. Remind me that You're never really gone.

Amen.

My Notes & Prayers

_____

_____

_____

_____

_____

_____

_____

_____

_____

_____

_____

_____

_____

_____

DAY 19: Praying Boldly

Key Verse
"Let us then approach God's throne of grace with confidence, so that we may receive mercy and find grace to help us in our time of need." —
Hebrews 4:16 (NIV)

Devotional Thought
Sometimes it feels like you have to have the right words, the perfect attitude, or be "good enough" to talk to God. But God isn't looking for perfect prayers—He's looking for your heart. Hebrews 4:16 invites you to come to God with confidence—boldly, not because of who you are, but because of who Jesus is. Because of Him, you don't have to tiptoe into God's presence. You can run in, knowing that love, grace, and mercy are waiting for you.

Praying boldly means you believe God hears you. It means you trust that He cares about even the small things. And it means you know your voice matters to Him.

So go ahead—talk to God about your dreams, your fears, your mistakes, your questions. Don't hold back. You are His daughter, and He delights in hearing from you.

Reflect

- What keeps you from praying with boldness, and how can you begin approaching God more confidently?
- If you truly believed God was listening and cared deeply, what would you talk to Him about today?

Prayer Moment

God, thank You for inviting me to come to You with confidence. Help me let go of fear, guilt, or shame and remember that I'm always welcome in Your presence. Give me boldness to speak to You honestly and trust that You are listening. Amen.

My Notes & Prayers

_____

_____

_____

_____

_____

_____

_____

_____

_____

_____

_____

_____

_____

_____

DAY 20: Being Still

Key Verse

"He says, 'Be still, and know that I am God; I will be exalted among the nations, I will be exalted in the earth.'" — Psalm 46:10 (NIV)

Devotional Thought

Life moves fast. Between school, texts, notifications, and everything pulling at your attention, it's easy to get caught up in the noise. But God invites you to something different: to be still.

Being still doesn't mean doing nothing. It means pressing pause. It means quieting the noise around you—and inside you—so you can hear His voice, feel His presence, and remember that He's God and you're not.

Stillness creates space for peace to grow. It reminds you that your worth isn't in how much you do, but in who you belong to. When you're still, you remember that God is in control—and He's got you.

In a world that's always rushing, stillness is a holy rebellion. It's how you reconnect with the One who holds everything together, including you.

Reflect
- When was the last time you slowed down to just be still with God? How can you make space for that today?
- What distractions can you lay down so you can listen more closely to God's voice?

Prayer Moment
God, help me slow down. Quiet my heart and remind me that You are God. I don't need to rush, prove, or worry. Teach me to rest in Your presence and trust that You are working, even when I'm still. Amen.

My Notes & Prayers

_____

_____

_____

_____

_____

_____

_____

_____

_____

_____

_____

_____

_____

_____

DAY 21: Following Jesus Daily

Key Verse
"Then he said to them all: 'Whoever wants to be my disciple must deny themselves and take up their cross daily and follow me.'" — Luke 9:23 (NIV)

Devotional Thought
Following Jesus isn't a one-time decision—it's a daily choice. Every morning, you get to decide: Will I follow my feelings, my fears, or will I follow Him?

Jesus doesn't call you to a perfect life—He calls you to a surrendered one. That means putting aside your own way of doing things and trusting that His way is better, even when it's hard. Taking up your cross daily means choosing love over pride, grace over gossip, and truth over popularity.

It's not always easy, but it's always worth it. Because when you follow Jesus, you walk in purpose, freedom, and deep joy. You walk with the One who knows you, loves you, and leads you exactly where you need to go.

You don't have to be perfect to follow Him—you just have to be willing.

Reflect
- What does following Jesus look like in your everyday life—at school, at home, or with friends?
- What is one thing you can surrender today to follow Him more fully?

Prayer Moment
Jesus, help me choose You every day. Teach me what it means to follow You, even when it's hard. Show me how to live with love, courage, and obedience. I want my life to reflect You. Amen.

My Notes & Prayers

_____

_____

_____

_____

_____

_____

_____

_____

_____

_____

_____

_____

_____

Weekly Check-in

How I felt this week, _____

_____

_____

_____

_____

_____

_____

_____

_____

_____

_____

_____

_____

Faith Activity: The "Faith Jar"

Purpose

To visually build trust by remembering how God has come through before—and believing He will again.

Supplies Needed

- A jar or small container (you can decorate it)
- Small slips of paper or notecards
- Pens/markers
- Optional: ribbon, labels, stickers to decorate

Instructions

1. Label the Jar:
2. Write "My Faith Jar" or "God Is Faithful" on your jar.
3. Fill It With Truth:
   - On each slip of paper, write down a time when God helped you, answered a prayer, gave you peace, or taught you something.
   - You can also write Bible verses about faith and trust (like Hebrews 11:1, Psalm 56:3, or Isaiah 26:3).
4. Add As You Go:

- Every time something happens that grows your faith—big or small—write it down and add it to the jar.
- Look Back When You Doubt:
- On tough days, pull out a few slips and remind yourself: God was faithful before. He'll be faithful again.

Bonus Journal Prompt:
"What has God done in my life that proves He is trustworthy?"

My Notes & Prayers

_____

_____

_____

_____

_____

_____

_____

_____

_____

_____

_____

_____

_____

WEEK 4:

PURPOSE

"Before I was born the Lord called me; from my mother's womb he has spoken my name."
—Isaiah 49:1 (NIV)

DAY 22: You Were Made for a Reason

Key Verse

"For we are God's handiwork, created in Christ Jesus to do good works, which God prepared in advance for us to do." — Ephesians 2:10 (NIV)

Devotional Thought

You weren't made by accident. You are God's handiwork—His masterpiece. That means you're not random, and your life isn't meaningless. God created you with a purpose that only you can fulfill.

Before you were even born, God had good things in mind for you to do. You don't have to earn your value or prove your worth. It's already been spoken over you by the One who made you. Your purpose might not always feel big or flashy. Sometimes it looks like encouraging a friend, standing up for someone who feels left out, or being kind when no one else is. But don't underestimate what God can do through a willing heart.

You were made for a reason—and every day is a new chance to walk in that truth.

Even when you don't feel "special," remember: God doesn't make mistakes.

Reflect
- What gifts, passions, or dreams has God placed in your heart that point to your purpose?
- How can you use who you are to make a difference in someone's life today?
-

Prayer Moment
God, thank You for creating me on purpose and for a purpose. Help me believe that I am Your masterpiece and that my life matters. Show me how to walk in the good things You've prepared for me. Amen.

My Notes & Prayers

_____

_____

_____

_____

_____

_____

_____

_____

_____

_____

_____

_____

_____

_____

DAY 23: Using Your Gifts

Key Verse

"There are different kinds of gifts, but the same Spirit distributes them.

There are different kinds of service, but the same Lord.
There are different kinds of working, but in all of them and in everyone it is the same God at work."
— 1 Corinthians 12:4–7 (NIV)

Devotional Thought

You don't have to be like everyone else to make a difference. God has given you unique gifts—special abilities, passions, and strengths—that He wants to use in powerful ways.

Maybe you're creative, a good listener, great at helping, or bold in speaking up. Whatever your gifts are, they were given on purpose for a purpose. You're not meant to hide them or compare them to others—you're meant to use them to shine God's light in the world.

Sometimes your gifts will feel big. Other times, they'll feel small. But when you offer them to God, nothing is small. The same Spirit who gave you your gifts is the one who works through them. You just need to say "yes."

So don't wait until you're older, more confident, or feel ready. God is ready now—and He's ready to work through you.

Reflect
- What are some of your God-given gifts or talents, and how can you use them to serve others?
- What's one small step you can take today to use your gifts for God's glory?

Prayer Moment
Lord, thank You for the gifts You've placed inside me. Help me to recognize them, not compare them, and use them to serve others. Give me courage to offer what I have, knowing that You can do amazing things through it. Amen.

___ / ___ / ___

My Notes & Prayers

_____
_____
_____
_____
_____
_____
_____
_____
_____
_____
_____
_____
_____
_____

DAY 24: Being a Light

Key Verse

"You are the light of the world. A town built on a hill cannot be hidden.
Neither do people light a lamp and put it under a bowl. Instead they put it on its stand, and it gives light to everyone in the house.
In the same way, let your light shine before others, that they may see your good deeds and glorify your Father in heaven."— Matthew 5:14–16 (NIV)

Devotional Thought

There's something beautiful about light—it shines, it warms, it guides. And Jesus says you are the light of the world.

That means wherever you go—school, your home, online—you carry the light of Jesus with you. You may not always feel bright, but when you choose love over hate, kindness over cruelty, and truth over lies, you shine.

Your light doesn't have to be loud to be powerful. Sometimes it's a smile, an encouraging word, a silent prayer, or standing up for what's right.

God placed His light in you not to be hidden, but to bring hope to others.

So don't dim your light to fit in.

The world needs what you carry. Shine boldly —not for attention, but to point people to Jesus.

Reflect

- How can you shine God's light in your school, friendships, or family?
- What are some ways you can let your light shine in your daily life?
- How can your actions reflect God's love to the people around you?

Prayer Moment

Jesus, thank You for calling me the light of the world. Help me shine bright for You, not for approval, but to show others Your love. Use my life to bring hope, kindness, and truth wherever I go.

Amen.

My Notes & Prayers

_____

_____

_____

_____

_____

_____

_____

_____

_____

_____

_____

_____

_____

_____

DAY 25: Being a Friend Like Jesus

Key Verse

"My command is this: Love each other as I have loved you.
Greater love has no one than this: to lay down one's life for one's friends." — John 15:12–13 (NIV)

Devotional Thought

Friendship is one of God's sweetest gifts. And Jesus shows us what real friendship looks like: it's selfless, kind, loyal, and full of love. He didn't just talk about love—He lived it.

Being a friend like Jesus means putting others first. It means listening, encouraging, forgiving, and being there—even when it's inconvenient. It's not always easy, but it's always worth it.

You won't be a perfect friend (none of us are), but when you choose to love others the way Jesus loves you, you bring light into their lives. And here's something powerful: God may use you to remind someone else that they're not alone.

So today, be the kind of friend who reflects the heart of Jesus. Because the world needs more friends like you.

Reflect

- How can you be a better friend to someone this week?
- What does it look like to love your friends the way Jesus loves you?
- Who in your life needs a reminder today that they are seen, loved, and not alone?

Prayer Moment

Jesus, thank You for being the best friend I could ever have. Teach me how to be a friend like You—kind, forgiving, and full of love. Help me to see others the way You see them and to love without holding back. Amen.

My Notes & Prayers

_____

_____

_____

_____

_____

_____

_____

_____

_____

_____

_____

_____

_____

_____

DAY 26: Courage to Stand Out

Key Verse

"Do not conform to the pattern of this world, but be transformed by the renewing of your mind. Then you will be able to test and approve what God's will is—his good, pleasing and perfect will." — Romans 12:2 (NIV)

Devotional Thought

It's easy to want to fit in—to wear what everyone else wears, say what everyone else says, and follow what everyone else follows. But God didn't create you to blend in. He made you to stand out.

Standing out doesn't mean being better—it means being different for the right reasons. It means choosing kindness when gossip is easier. It means holding onto your faith when others walk away. It means being bold enough to follow Jesus, even when it's unpopular.

The world will always try to shape you, but God wants to transform you—from the inside out.

He wants your heart, your thoughts, your choices to reflect His truth, not the world's opinions. It takes courage to stand out. But when you do, you show others that it's okay to live for something greater—Someone greater.

Reflect

- In what area of your life do you feel pressure to conform, and how can you choose to stand out for God instead?
- What truth from God's Word gives you the strength to live differently?

Prayer Moment

God, give me the courage to stand out for You. Help me not to follow the crowd but to follow Christ. Renew my mind with Your truth and teach me how to live boldly, even when it's hard. I want my life to honor You.

Amen.

My Notes & Prayers

_____

_____

_____

_____

_____

_____

_____

_____

_____

_____

_____

_____

_____

_____

DAY 27: God Can Use You Now

Key Verse

"Don't let anyone look down on you because you are young, but set an example for the believers in speech, in conduct, in love, in faith and in purity." — 1 Timothy 4:12 (NIV)

Devotional Thought

You don't have to wait until you're older, smarter, or more "spiritual" to be used by God. If you've said "yes" to Jesus, then you're already qualified to shine for Him—right now. Paul reminded Timothy that even though he was young, he could still be a powerful example to others.

The same is true for you. Your words, your attitude, your choices—they all speak. And when they reflect Jesus, they make a difference.

Don't let doubts, fear, or others' opinions stop you from stepping into your purpose. Age isn't a limit for God—it's a launchpad. He loves using young people to do bold, world-changing things.

So speak up. Live with love. Trust God fully. Be an example not just someday, but today.

Reflect

- What lie have you believed about needing to wait before God can use you—and what does God say instead?
- In what area of your life can you be an example of Jesus to others this week?

Prayer Moment

Lord, thank You for reminding me that I don't have to wait to be used by You. Help me to be an example in how I speak, act, and love. Use me right now—just as I am—to show others who You are. Amen.

My Notes & Prayers

_____

_____

_____

_____

_____

_____

_____

_____

_____

_____

_____

_____

_____

_____

DAY 28: Staying Strong When It's Hard

Key Verse

"Let us not become weary in doing good, for at the proper time we will reap a harvest if we do not give up." — Galatians 6:9 (NIV)

Devotional Thought

There are days when everything feels heavy—when doing the right thing seems like the hardest thing. Maybe you're the only one in your friend group standing up for what's right, or you're trying to stay positive when life feels unfair. It can feel tiring when no one notices or when others don't do the same. God sees your struggle and your faithfulness. He sees every act of kindness, every prayer, every time you choose Him over the crowd.

He knows it's not easy, but He promises that your perseverance has a purpose.
Staying strong doesn't mean you never get tired or discouraged—it means you don't quit. It means trusting God even when it's hard to see how things will turn out. Remember, you're not doing this alone.

The Holy Spirit gives you strength when yours runs low.
Keep going. You're planting seeds that will grow.

Reflect
- What's something good you've been doing that feels hard to keep up? How can you stay strong?
- When have you felt like giving up, and what helped you keep going?
- What promise from God can you hold onto during hard times?

Prayer Moment
Dear God, sometimes I feel so tired of doing the right thing when it feels like no one notices or cares. Help me stay strong and keep trusting You, even when life is tough. Remind me that You see every choice I make and that nothing I do for You is wasted. Give me the strength to keep going, knowing that You're walking with me every step of the way.

Amen.

My Notes & Prayers

_____

_____

_____

_____

_____

_____

_____

_____

_____

_____

_____

_____

_____

_____

DAY 29: Living with Joy

Key Verse
"Do not grieve, for the joy of the Lord is your strength." — Nehemiah 8:10b (NIV)

Devotional Thought
Joy isn't the same as happiness. Happiness can fade when circumstances change, but joy goes deeper. It comes from knowing God is with you, loves you, and is working everything for your good—even when things aren't perfect. Joy is rooted in who God is, not in what's happening around you.

The people in Nehemiah's day were crying when they realized how far they had wandered from God. But instead of staying in their sadness, Nehemiah reminded them to celebrate. Why? Because returning to God is worth rejoicing over. The joy of the Lord isn't based on your perfection—it's based on His presence.

Let His joy be your strength today. Smile because you are loved. Laugh because God holds your future.

Rejoice because your story isn't over yet.

Reflect
- What's something in your life right now that brings you godly joy?
- How can you choose joy even when things don't go your way?

Prayer Moment
Father, Thank You for the kind of joy that doesn't depend on my circumstances. Fill my heart with Your joy today. Help me to choose joy even when things feel hard or uncertain. Let Your joy be my strength and help me shine that joy to others. I want to live with a smile that comes from knowing You love me and are always near.

Amen.

My Notes & Prayers

_____

_____

_____

_____

_____

_____

_____

_____

_____

_____

_____

_____

_____

_____

DAY 30: Finishing the Race

Key Verse

"I have fought the good fight, I have finished the race, I have kept the faith." — 2 Timothy 4:7 (NIV)

Devotional Thought

You've made it to Day 30! That's no small thing. Just like Paul, you're learning what it means to keep going, to hold on to your faith, and to stay committed to Jesus—even when life is full of twists and turns.

God never asked for perfection. He wants your faithfulness. Your journey won't always be easy, but every step you take with Jesus matters. Keep running your race with courage, trusting that He's right beside you. And when you fall, don't stay down—get back up. The finish line is worth it.

Life is a journey, not a sprint.

This is only the beginning of your walk with Him.

You were made for this race, and God has equipped you with everything you need to finish strong.

Reflect

- What helps you keep going in your walk with Jesus when things get hard?
- What does "finishing the race" look like in your daily life?
- What have you learned through this 30-day journey with God?

Prayer Moment

Lord, Thank You for walking with me through this journey. I know there's still more ahead, but I want to keep running my race with faith and courage. Help me to stay focused on You and not give up when things get hard. Strengthen my heart to finish strong and live each day for Your glory. I trust You with my story, and I'm excited for what's next.

Amen.

My Notes & Prayers

_____

_____

_____

_____

_____

_____

_____

_____

_____

_____

_____

_____

_____

_____

Weekly Check-in

How I felt this week, _____

_____

_____

_____

_____

_____

_____

_____

_____

_____

_____

_____

_____

Purpose Activity: "Designed On Purpose"

Vision Board

Theme Verse:

"For we are God's handiwork, created in Christ Jesus to do good works, which God prepared in advance for us to do."— Ephesians 2:10 (NIV)

Purpose:

To help girls explore the unique gifts, dreams, and values God has placed in their hearts and connect them to His bigger purpose.

Supplies Needed:

- Poster board or large cardstock
- Old magazines, newspapers, printouts, or drawings
- Scissors, glue sticks, markers, stickers, washi tape, etc.
- Bible verse printables (optional)

Instructions:

1. Title Your Board:
2. At the top of the board, write "God's Purpose for Me" or "Created on Purpose."
3. Reflect First (Optional Journal Prompts):
   - What am I passionate about?
   - What are some gifts or talents God has given me?

- Who do I love to help or serve?
- What makes me feel most alive?

- **Build Your Vision Board:**
  - Cut or draw images, words, and quotes that represent your God-given interests, dreams, and identity.
  - Include Bible verses that remind you of God's purpose for your life (e.g., Jeremiah 29:11, Proverbs 19:21, 1 Peter 4:10).
  - Add drawings, prayers, or pictures of people who inspire you.
- **Purpose Prayer** (optional):
- Write a short prayer on your board:
- "God, thank You for creating me with purpose. Help me walk in the plans You have for me."
- Share (Optional):
- Share one meaningful part of their vision board with the group or write a short reflection about what they discovered.

Follow-Up Idea:

Keep your board somewhere you will see daily as a reminder that you are created on purpose, for a purpose.

My Notes & Prayers

_____

_____

_____

_____

_____

_____

_____

_____

_____

_____

_____

_____

_____

_____

10 Bonus Devotions

*"For I am convinced that neither death nor life,
neither angels nor demons, neither the present
nor the future, nor any powers,
neither height nor depth, nor anything else in all
creation, will be able to separate us from the love
of God that is in Christ Jesus our Lord."*
Romans 8:38–39 (NIV)

Love: Loved First

Key Verse

"We love because He first loved us." – 1 John 4:19 (NIV)

Devotional Thought

Before you ever prayed your first prayer, said your first word, or made your first mistake—God already loved you.

His love doesn't depend on how popular you are, how you look, how well you perform, or whether you feel like you "deserve" it. It's a pure, steady, never-giving-up kind of love—the kind that doesn't change based on moods, mistakes, or moments.

In a world where love is often used as a reward or something to earn, God flips the script. He loved you first. That means you don't have to chase it, perform for it, or try to prove you're good enough. You're already loved—completely, unconditionally, and eternally. And here's the beautiful part: when you understand that you are fully loved, you can begin to love others from a place of confidence, not insecurity.

You no longer have to compare yourself to others, because God's love for you is personal and perfect.

You can forgive more freely, speak more kindly, and give more generously—because you're not running on empty. You're living loved.
So today, rest in this truth:
You are loved.
You are chosen.
You are enough—because He is enough.

Reflect
- When do you feel tempted to chase love or try to earn it?
- How can remembering that God loved you first change the way you see yourself and others?

Prayer Moment

Dear God, Thank You for loving me first. Not because I earned it, but simply because You are love. Sometimes I feel like I'm not enough—like I have to try harder or be better to be loved. But today, I choose to believe the truth: that I am fully known and fully loved by You. Let that love sink deep into my heart. Help me stop chasing approval and start living from the love You've already given me. Teach me to love others the way You love me—with patience, grace, and kindness. Thank You for being the kind of love I can always count on.

In Jesus' name, Amen.

My Notes & Prayers

_____

_____

_____

_____

_____

_____

_____

_____

_____

_____

_____

_____

_____

_____

Real Love

Key Verse
"Love is patient, love is kind. It does not envy, it does not boast, it is not proud..." – 1 Corinthians 13:4 (NIV)

Devotional Thought
The world throws around the word "love" a lot. You hear it in songs, see it in movies, and read it in texts—"I love this outfit!" "I love him!" "I love tacos!" But real love—God's kind of love— is way deeper than a feeling. It's a commitment to care for someone the way God cares for us.

In 1 Corinthians 13, we see the clearest picture of what love truly looks like. It's not selfish, dramatic, or controlling. It's patient when others are slow, kind when it's easier to snap, humble when pride tries to win. Love doesn't keep score, get jealous, or give up when things get tough.

This kind of love starts with God. He is love, and when we know Him, we can love others better—friends, family, even ourselves. Loving like Jesus doesn't mean being perfect; it means choosing to reflect His heart in a world that desperately needs it.

Reflect

- **H**ow is God's definition of love different from what you see on social media or in relationships around you?
- Which part of 1 Corinthians 13:4–7 do you want to grow in most?
-

Prayer Moment

Jesus, teach me how to love like You. Help me be patient, kind, and humble—even when it's hard. I want to understand Your love so I can live it out every day.

Amen.

My Notes & Prayers

_____

_____

_____

_____

_____

_____

_____

_____

_____

_____

_____

_____

_____

_____

Purity: Guarding Your Heart

Key Verse

"Above all else, guard your heart, for everything you do flows from it." – Proverbs 4:23 (NIV)

Devotional Thought

When you hear the word "purity," what comes to mind? For many, it's often tied to rules about what not to do. But God's view of purity is so much more than a list of don'ts—it's about protecting what matters most: your heart.

Your heart is where your dreams, decisions, and beliefs live. It's the part of you that feels deeply, trusts deeply, and loves deeply. That's why Proverbs tells us to guard it "above all else." Not with walls, but with wisdom. When you choose purity—whether in your words, relationships, music, thoughts, or boundaries—you're not limiting yourself. You're protecting the beauty of who you are in Christ.

The world might tell you that purity is outdated or unnecessary. But the truth is, when you live purely, you're walking in freedom. You're saying, "God, I trust Your way over mine."

Purity isn't about being perfect. It's about living with purpose, honoring God with your body, mind, and spirit—and choosing what fills you with peace, not regret.

Reflect

- What are some areas where you need to set stronger boundaries to guard your heart?
- How can you invite God to help you stay pure in your thoughts, friendships, and media choices?

Prayer Moment

Dear God, Thank You for creating my heart with so much value. Help me to guard it with wisdom, not fear. I want to live purely—not to be perfect, but to please You and protect the good You've placed in me. Give me strength when I'm tempted and courage when I need to walk away. Show me how to set boundaries and stay true to who You say I am. In Jesus' name,

Amen.

My Notes & Prayers

_____

_____

_____

_____

_____

_____

_____

_____

_____

_____

_____

_____

_____

_____

Wisdom: God's Way Is Wiser

Key Verse

"If any of you lacks wisdom, you should ask God, who gives generously to all without finding fault, and it will be given to you." – James 1:5 (NIV)

Devotional Thought

Have you ever faced a decision and thought, "I have no idea what to do"? Maybe it was a friendship issue, a temptation, a future goal, or even just how to respond to a hard text. In moments like that, we don't just need advice—we need wisdom. And not just any wisdom—God's wisdom.

The amazing part? God says if you ask Him for wisdom, He'll give it generously—without judging you for not having it all together. That means you can be real with God, admit when you don't know, and trust that He'll help you see things clearly.

Wisdom is different from knowledge. You can know a lot and still make bad choices. Wisdom helps you know how to live, when to wait, when to speak, and when to walk away.

God's wisdom always leads you toward peace, purpose, and truth. It won't always be the easiest choice, but it will always be the best one in the long run.

So next time you're unsure, pause and pray. Ask for wisdom. Read God's Word. Talk to a trusted adult or mentor. And listen for God's gentle direction. He wants to guide your life in ways that protect you, grow you, and prepare you for His plans.

Reflect:

- What's a decision you're facing right now that you need God's wisdom for?
- How can you practice asking God for wisdom before making choices instead of after?

Prayer Moment:

God, I admit I don't always know what to do or which path to take. I need Your wisdom to guide me in the big decisions and the everyday ones. Help me recognize Your voice above all the noise. Give me a heart that listens, waits, and obeys—even when it's hard. I want to walk in Your ways because I trust that You see what I can't. Thank You for giving wisdom so freely when I ask. In Jesus' name,

Amen.

My Notes & Prayers

_____

_____

_____

_____

_____

_____

_____

_____

_____

_____

_____

_____

_____

_____

Peer Pressure: Standing Strong

Key Verse

"Do not be misled: 'Bad company corrupts good character.'" – 1 Corinthians 15:33 (NIV)

Devotional Thought

Let's be real—fitting in can feel like everything. You want to belong. You want friends. You want to feel accepted. That's normal. But sometimes, the pressure to be liked can push you to do things you know aren't right.

Peer pressure doesn't always look like someone daring you to do something wrong. It can be more subtle—laughing at something that makes you uncomfortable, pretending to agree with things you don't believe in, or staying silent when you know you should speak up.

But God calls you to something higher. He calls you to stand strong, even when it's hard. Even when you're the only one doing the right thing. Being different takes courage, but you're not alone.

God is with you, and He's given you the strength through His Spirit to say no, walk away, or stand up. Your character—who you are when no one's watching—matters more than the approval of people who may not truly see your worth.

Surround yourself with friends who build you up, not ones who pressure you to compromise. And remember: every time you choose to honor God over popularity, you're growing stronger, bolder, and more rooted in your faith. You don't need to be who others expect you to be. You were made to stand out.

Reflect

- What's one area of your life where you've felt pressure to blend in or go along with the crowd?
- How can you prepare your heart and mind to stand strong in those moments?

Prayer Moment

Dear God, It's hard to go against the crowd. Sometimes I just want to fit in, even when I know it means compromising what I believe. But I want to be strong. I want to be the kind of girl who stands for You—even when it's lonely or awkward. Give me the courage to walk away when I need to. Help me choose friends who love You and push me closer to You. When I feel weak, remind me that You're right beside me, and I don't have to face pressure on my own. Teach me to value Your approval more than anyone else's. Thank You for making me bold and brave in You. In Jesus' name,

Amen.

My Notes & Prayers

_____

_____

_____

_____

_____

_____

_____

_____

_____

_____

_____

_____

_____

_____

Honoring Your Parents: A Heart Posture

Key Verse

"Honor your father and your mother, so that you may live long in the land the Lord your God is giving you." – Exodus 20:12 (NIV)

Devotional Thought

Let's be honest—honoring your parents isn't always easy. They don't always understand what you're going through. They might say "no" when you really want a "yes." Sometimes they're strict, embarrassing, or even just plain frustrating. But here's the thing: honoring your parents isn't about pretending they're perfect. It's about choosing respect—because God says it's important.

Honoring your parents starts with your heart. It shows up in your attitude, your words, and how you respond—even when you disagree. It's not just about following rules; it's about trusting that God put your parents in your life for a purpose. Yes, they make mistakes. But they also carry a responsibility to guide, protect, and love you.

When you choose to honor them, you're not just doing something kind—you're obeying God. And He promises that it leads to blessing. That doesn't mean everything will be perfect, but it does mean God sees your obedience and rewards it with peace, wisdom, and growth. And honoring doesn't have to be complicated. It can look like listening without rolling your eyes, helping without being asked, or simply saying "thank you." Even small things matter when done with the right heart.

Remember, your relationship with your parents shapes how you relate to other authority figures—and even how you relate to God. Start with small steps today, and ask God to help you grow in love and respect for the ones He's placed over you.

Reflect
- What's one way you can honor your parents this week, even if it feels hard?
- How does honoring your parents strengthen your relationship with God?

Prayer Moment

Dear God, Thank You for giving me parents who care about me, even when I don't always understand their choices. Sometimes I get frustrated or feel like they don't see things from my side. But I want to honor them because You ask me to.

Help me to have a heart that respects them—even when we don't agree. Give me patience when I feel misunderstood and humility when I want to argue. Teach me to show love in my words and actions. Let my obedience to You shine through how I treat them.

Thank You for being a perfect Father who leads me in love and truth.

In Jesus' name,

    Amen.

My Notes & Prayers

_____

_____

_____

_____

_____

_____

_____

_____

_____

_____

_____

_____

_____

_____

Vanity: More Than What You See

Key Verse

"Your beauty should not come from outward adornment... Rather, it should be that of your inner self, the unfading beauty of a gentle and quiet spirit, which is of great worth in God's sight." – 1 Peter 3:3–4 (NIV)

Devotional Thought

Everywhere you look—social media, ads, magazines—there's pressure to be prettier, trendier, and more "put together."It's easy to fall into the trap of thinking that how you look is the most important part of who you are. But God says something very different.

God sees your heart, not just your highlight reel. He's not impressed by perfect skin or the latest outfits—He's drawn to kindness, humility, honesty, and love. True beauty isn't filtered or photoshopped. It's the kind that shines from within and reflects His image.

There's nothing wrong with wanting to look nice or take care of yourself, but vanity becomes a problem when it takes God's place in your heart.

When we're more focused on being admired than being transformed, we lose sight of who we were created to be.

Here's the truth: You are already beautiful because you were created by a beautiful God. You don't need to compete, compare, or chase after attention. Your worth isn't tied to how others see you—it's anchored in how God sees you, and He calls you His masterpiece.
So today, ask yourself: am I spending more time trying to impress people or connect with God? Because only one of those leads to lasting joy.

Reflect

- What are some ways you've felt pressured to focus more on how you look than who you are?
- How can you shift your focus to grow your inner beauty—the kind that matters to God?

Prayer Moment

Dear God, sometimes I feel caught up in appearances. I compare myself to others and wonder if I measure up. But You remind me that real beauty starts on the inside. Help me not to chase attention or be defined by what the world calls beautiful. Instead, make my heart gentle, kind, and strong in You.

Let my confidence come from knowing I'm Your daughter. Shape me into a girl who reflects Your love in how I think, speak, and live. Thank You for creating me wonderfully and purposefully—just as I am.

In Jesus' name,

Amen.

My Notes & Prayers

_____

_____

_____

_____

_____

_____

_____

_____

_____

_____

_____

_____

_____

_____

Humility: Quiet Strength

Key Verse

"God opposes the proud but shows favor to the humble." – James 4:6 (NIV)

Devotional Thought

In a world that shouts, "Look at me!", humility whispers, "Look at God." Humility isn't about putting yourself down or pretending you're not good at anything. It's about knowing who you are—and who you're not—and trusting God to be the center of your story.

Being humble means recognizing that every gift you have—your personality, talents, creativity, intelligence—is from God. You don't have to brag or prove anything, because you know your worth comes from Him. It's a quiet confidence that doesn't need the spotlight to shine.

Humility also means being teachable. It's being willing to say, "I was wrong" or "I need help." That takes more strength than pride ever could. Pride puts up walls. Humility opens doors—to deeper friendships, wiser decisions, and a stronger relationship with God.

Jesus is our perfect example of humility.

Even though He was the Son of God, He washed feet, served others, and gave His life for people who didn't deserve it. When we live like Him—serving instead of showing off—we stand out in all the right ways.

You were made to live boldly and confidently, but not pridefully. Let your light shine—but always remember where that light comes from.

Reflect
- In what areas of your life do you feel tempted to seek attention or prove yourself?
- What's one way you can practice humility in your relationships this week?

Prayer Moment

Dear God, Thank You for loving me, not because I'm perfect, but because I'm Yours. I want to be confident, but not prideful. Help me to walk in humility like Jesus did—to serve others, admit when I'm wrong, and remember that everything good in me comes from You. Teach me to put others before myself, not to be praised, but to reflect Your heart. Let my strength come from depending on You, not from trying to impress anyone else.

In Jesus' name,

Amen.

My Notes & Prayers

_____

_____

_____

_____

_____

_____

_____

_____

_____

_____

_____

_____

_____

_____

Fruit of the Spirit: Growing from the Inside Out

Key Verse

"But the fruit of the Spirit is love, joy, peace, patience, kindness, goodness, faithfulness, gentleness and self-control." – Galatians 5:22–23 (NIV)

Devotional Thought

If your life were a tree, what kind of fruit would people see?

Would they find kindness in your words? Patience in your reactions? Joy, even on hard days? The fruit of the Spirit is a picture of what grows in your life when you let God lead your heart. These nine traits aren't just rules to follow—they're evidence that you're walking with Jesus.

But here's the thing: fruit doesn't grow overnight. You won't magically become more patient or joyful just because you want to. It takes time.

Growth happens when you spend time with God, read His Word, and ask the Holy Spirit to shape your heart. It's a process, not perfection.

And just like a tree needs sunlight, water, and strong roots, your faith needs time in prayer, worship, and community. You won't always get it right—and that's okay. God isn't expecting perfection. He's looking for a heart that says, "Yes, grow me."
So instead of trying to look perfect on the outside, focus on what's happening on the inside. When the Spirit is alive in you, the fruit will come—and it will bless everyone around you.

Reflect

- Which fruit of the Spirit do you feel strongest in right now?
- Which one is hardest for you, and how can you ask God to help you grow in it?

Prayer Moment

Dear God, Thank You for planting good things in me through Your Spirit. I want my life to show love, joy, peace, patience, kindness, goodness, faithfulness, gentleness, and self-control—but sometimes I fall short. Grow these things in me from the inside out.

Help me to stay close to You so that Your Spirit can keep shaping my heart. Make me a girl who reflects Your character in how I live, speak, and treat others. Even when it's hard, help me keep growing.

In Jesus' name,

Amen.

My Notes & Prayers

_____

_____

_____

_____

_____

_____

_____

_____

_____

_____

_____

_____

_____

Armor of God: Dressed for Battle

Key Verse

*"Put on the full armor of God, so that you can take your stand against the devil's schemes." –
Ephesians 6:11 (NIV)*

Devotional Thought

Let's face it—life can feel like a battle. There are temptations, lies, doubts, and moments where you just feel spiritually exhausted. But God didn't leave you defenseless. He gave you armor—not physical armor, but spiritual strength to protect your heart, mind, and soul. Here's what your armor looks like:

- Belt of Truth – Know who God is and what He says is true about you.
- Breastplate of Righteousness – Guard your heart by living right and choosing what honors God.
- Shoes of Peace – Walk confidently, knowing God is with you wherever you go.
- Shield of Faith – Trust God even when you can't see the outcome. Your faith blocks lies and fears.
- Helmet of Salvation – Protect your mind with the truth that you belong to Jesus.

- Sword of the Spirit – This is the Word of God. Read it, know it, use it!

When you "put on" the armor of God, you're saying, "I'm not fighting alone. I'm standing in God's strength." It doesn't mean life will be easy, but it does mean you're equipped for the battle. Every time you read your Bible, pray, resist temptation, or speak truth, you're using your armor.

So don't leave your armor in the corner—put it on daily. You are stronger than you think when you stand with God.

Reflect
- Which piece of the armor do you think you need the most right now—and why?
- What's one way you can "put on your armor" each morning before you start the day?

Prayer Moment

Dear God, Thank You for giving me everything I need to stand strong. Life can be hard, and sometimes I feel weak, but I know that with Your armor, I can face anything. Help me to hold on to Your truth, walk in Your peace, and stand firm in faith.

Remind me daily that I don't have to fight alone. Strengthen me with Your Word, protect my heart, and guide my steps. I want to be a girl who walks boldly with You, fully dressed for battle.

In Jesus' name,

Amen.

My Notes & Prayers

_____

_____

_____

_____

_____

_____

_____

_____

_____

_____

_____

_____

_____

_____

Activity: Secret Serve Challenge

Instructions:

1. Choose one person in your life—maybe a parent, teacher, classmate, or friend—who you can serve without telling them it was you.
2. Do something kind or helpful:
   - Write them an anonymous note of encouragement
   - Clean or organize something without being asked
   - Leave a small gift or Bible verse somewhere they'll find it
   - Speak kindly about them behind their back (yes, that counts!)
3. Don't post about it. Don't take credit. Just let your action be between you and God.

Reflection Questions:

- How did it feel to serve someone without being noticed or praised?
- What did you learn about your heart and attitude through this challenge?

My Notes & Prayers

_____

_____

_____

_____

_____

_____

_____

_____

_____

_____

_____

_____

_____

My Notes & Prayers

_____

_____

_____

_____

_____

_____

_____

_____

_____

_____

_____

_____

_____

_____

_____

My Notes & Prayers

My Notes & Prayers

_____ / / _____

My Notes & Prayers

_____

_____

_____

_____

_____

_____

_____

_____

_____

_____

_____

_____

_____

_____

My Notes & Prayers

_____

_____

_____

_____

_____

_____

_____

_____

_____

_____

_____

_____

_____

_____

My Notes & Prayers

_____

_____

_____

_____

_____

_____

_____

_____

_____

_____

_____

_____

_____

As you reach the end of this journey, remember:
You are cherished. You are chosen. You are called.

The truths you've embraced are not just for a month—they're for a lifetime.

Continue to seek God daily, lean into His promises, and walk confidently in the purpose He has for you.

Your story is still unfolding, and the best is yet to come. Stay rooted in His love,

Shabriya Hill O

About the Author

Shabriya Hill is a passionate writer, mentor, and speaker based in San Francisco, California. As a devoted mother and woman of unwavering faith, she is committed to empowering teen girls to discover their true identity in Christ. With a heart for mentorship and healing, Shabriya combines biblical truth with practical encouragement to inspire young women to live boldly, love authentically, and walk confidently in who God created them to be.

Her writing creates a safe and honest space for spiritual growth, emotional healing, and personal transformation. Whether through devotionals, workshops, or one-on-one mentorship, she helps young women embrace their worth, value their voices, and live out their God-given purpose.

Shabriya is the author of the debut book I Can't Turn Back: A Journey from Spiritual Displacement to Divine Redemption, a powerful testament to God's ability to restore, redeem, and realign our hearts with His calling. Through her story and ministry, she seeks to remind every girl that she is seen, known, and deeply loved by the One who created her.

www.ingramcontent.com/pod-product-compliance
Lightning Source LLC
Chambersburg PA
CBHW082226140626